Leaving Well for the organization: a navigation guide
for workplace transitions
Copyright © 2023 by Naomi Hattaway

8th & Home
Pompano Beach, FL
www.NaomiHattaway.com

Printed in the United States of America

Library of Congress Control Number: 2023913379

Author photo by Kamrin Baker
Cover design by Enoch Pugh
Page layout by Sarah Hartley

ISBN: 979-8-9886947-0-0
ISBN: 979-8-9886947-1-7

For more information, visit www.NaomiHattaway.com

Publisher's Cataloging-in-Publication Data
provided by Five Rainbows Cataloging Services

Names: Hattaway, Naomi Amanda, 1976- author.e
Title: Leaving well for the organization : a navigation guide for workplace
transitions / Naomi Hattaway.
Description: Pompano Beach, FL : 8th & Home, 2023. | Series: Leaving well,
bk. 1.
Identifiers: LCCN 2023913379 (print) | ISBN 979-8-9886947-0-0
(paperback) | ISBN 979-8-9886947-1-7 (ebook)
Subjects: LCSH: Employee retention. | Personnel management. | Career
changes. | Organizational change. | Management. | BISAC: BUSINESS
& ECONOMICS / Human Resources & Personnel Management. |
BUSINESS & ECONOMICS / Organizational Development. | BUSINESS
& ECONOMICS / Nonprofit Organizations & Charities / Management &
Leadership.
Classification: LCC HF5549.5.R58 H28 2023 (print) | LCC HF5549.5.R58
(ebook) | DDC 658.3/111--dc23.

CONTENTS

"When experiencing a life transition, everything changes: restructured days, shifted community, so many feelings. Leaving well is the art and practice of moving on from a place, thing, role, or job, with intention, purpose, and when possible: joy."

NAOMI HATTAWAY

People Leave

Resignations, terminations, transitions and other necessary endings are common challenges facing every organization. This is reality.

All too often, when people leave, a familiar cycle repeats: processes are not passed along properly and the remaining employees are impacted by new workloads, grief, and stress. Even when ample notices are given, they are often submitted without a plan for a seamless transition.

Another reality is that organizations hire new employees.

When this happens, how organizations handle and navigate transitions inevitably sets the stage for how new employees begin their experience with your organization, and your culture.

There are common traps in the onboarding and offboarding process of every organization across the country - *but it doesn't have to be this way.* **This book is an exploration of possibility.**

While specific answers and solutions will be based on the nuance and specific details of your organization, this book will offer new ways of thinking about the health of your teams and the staying power of your work and impact.

In this book, I will share practical ways to lean into leaving well as a part of your culture.

Consider whether you agree with any of the following:
- Leaving is hard.
- Retention feels even harder.
- You and your leadership team are good people.
- Your organization's mission is incredibly important.
- Culture and systems are critical to success.
- Your objectives and metrics are measured and necessary.
- At the end of the day, you want to serve your community.

The majority of these are likely true for your organization, and I'd argue that even with those truths, you have a culture problem in and amongst your team.

Many leaders focus on hiring, attracting diverse talent pools, and onboarding (insert the well-known book, The First 90 Days), yet do not address or highlight systemic and underlying problems that exist when employees leave.

Each person who leaves holds the potential to effect a loss of organizational impact, and also controls the level of disruption of your organization's presence in the community.

Thinking back to the last twelve months, how many exits have you had? In addition to the cycles of transition stress mentioned above, there are also time and money costs associated with the integration of any interim or new hire, including internal relationship and trust building. And all of this assumes a TYPICAL exit! The potential total loss and disruption of each person or project really begins to add up.

Meaning:

Your organization risks losing years of impact with each transition. Some of that loss is measurable. However, leaders today must also anticipate the unknown, against unrealized potential, hidden pitfalls, and nearly-invisible metrics such as "what could have been."

Given that obligation, it becomes clear that traditional hiring strategies ignore the obvious: it takes years for someone to find their footing in a new organization.

This fact understandably directs leaders to focus on improving onboarding. But what if we're asking the wrong questions here or starting at the wrong place? Clearing up the issues and challenges a new person will face in your organization begins with being intentional about how the last person was offboarded.

In other words: the way people leave is actually where change-making organizations should start problem-solving. We need to focus on the exits, and direct our efforts towards the Last 90 Days. One bad exit risks the downfall of your entire organizational structure, integrity, foundation, and reputation.

Leaving well is the art and practice of moving on from a place, thing, role, job, with intention, purpose, and when possible: joy.

The culture of leaving well protects your reputation, preserves and promotes the mental health of employees, and helps maintain professional relationships with your stakeholders. Organizations who embed leaving well into their work culture also acquire protection for organizational assets, and prioritize purposeful knowledge transfer.

What if your organization could address and embrace the inevitable process of transitions, without increasing attrition?

What if company loyalty was a thing of the past, and instead your teams and people felt cared for, during their tenure with your organization?

What if traditional succession planning became a thing of the past?

What if you never had to consider or worry about interim leadership again?

We avoid prioritizing leaving and endings in a healthy way, because we have never been taught how to navigate this leaving, well.

Leaving Well
for the Organization

Long before I started implementing this practice with client organizations, it was a very personal two-word phrase our family used each and every time we moved houses—which was a frequent occurrence, including multiple international moves.

My friend Jerry Jones introduced me to the phrase, and my family and I shaped its meaning. Every time we leave a city or town - which is pretty frequently, an average of every two years - we take a photo of our favorite locations and snap images to remind us of our time spent there.

We honor and acknowledge the place we are leaving and, even though it may sound strange, we mentally say goodbye to each room in the house and let the memories flood in. Every time we shift to a new city, we choose keepsakes from the places we leave, stop into each of our favorite restaurants to eat our favorite meals, and say goodbye to our most treasured librarians.

Over the last few years, I've learned that leaving well is not only useful for my personal life, but the same concepts transfer to the workplace. Leaving is inevitable. So if it's true for all of us, that we will one day leave our workplace, our jobs, our gigs, why do we avoid intentionally planning the way we leave?

For leaders inside social impact organizations, we might think that building a beautiful culture around "leaving well" might make people leave faster.

In personal/life situations, we avoid endings because we hope that our situation is fixable, or because we are scared of the future.

Often we don't realize the related stress levels that accompany prolonged staying are higher than those related to leaving. Sometimes we assume that conflict or drama will accompany decisions around leaving.

But what if being intentional about instituting and embodying a culture of leaving well actually allowed us to meet our organizational and personal goals in even better and faster ways?

We avoid prioritizing endings and leaving in a healthy way, because we have never been taught how to navigate this leaving, well.

Over the last ten years of working in the realm of organizational health, I have witnessed numerous transitions of executive leaders and CEOs. While much attention is often placed on the selection and onboarding of new leaders, the process of departing with grace and leaving a positive legacy is equally critical - and I argue that it is actually more important than the hire ever will be. The end is just the beginning.

My first experience of leaving well in the workplace was with the local affiliate of a large international non profit in the affordable housing sector. I joined the organization at a director level, with a large team reporting to me, across multiple departments, and also sat on the executive leadership team. Within a few weeks of joining the organization, I began seeing the correlation between location-based leaving well (such as moving or relocating a home) and organization-based leaving well.

While the organization was well-respected in the community, my department was floundering. The previous leader in my role was leaving with an ample notice period and on good terms. I was welcomed to the space with open arms and we spent time together as she onboarded me into the seat. However, it was clear once I officially stepped in, that the organizational health was lacking.

Over the next months, I implemented multiple new policies and embedded new culture building opportunities for my staff, and for the larger organization as a whole. Those included an in-depth customer journey map, and a follow-up services gap analysis, to better understand inefficiencies and missed opportunities for funding and improving services.

I instituted an exercise examining roles and duties, with concrete swimlanes established. We also prioritized updating the team's resumes as an intentional act of acknowledging that many of the staff had been there for many years, but without examining their current contribution to the organization, the larger system.

During a routine and required succession planning exercise, I was told I would be named as the deputy executive director, for the purpose of completing said exercise. While that checked the proverbial box for traditional organizational health actions, in reality, it did nothing to shore up the foundation of the organization. Systems were not examined, founder syndrome was left unchecked, and the structure and culture of business as usual was perpetuated.

When I subsequently left that organization, I implemented a purposeful knowledge transfer, orchestrated and planned intentional communication about the transition, and offered powerful accountability, all in the container of leaving well as I exited. It was this experience that launched my work in the space of leaving well consulting with individual leaders and organizations.

Imagine if organizations normalized these work endings, rather than focusing on them as a negative!

Imagine if organizations prioritized individual resources and support to prioritize leaving well each and every time we needed a new opportunity.

Leadership styles have long been examined and dissected. Books are plentiful on the topics of various methodologies of leadership, both personal leadership and on the topic of the art and act of leading organizations. Leaving well as a leadership model offers a powerful comprehensive structure that provides benefits to human capital and an organization's budget and bottom line, all ahead of the need . . . but only when practiced and embedded into organizational culture.

> *"When I surveyed more than 1300 senior HR leaders, almost 90% agreed that 'transitions into new roles are the most challenging times in the professional lives of leaders.' Nearly 3/4 agreed that 'success or failure during the first few months is a strong predictor of overall success or failure in the job.'"*
> -Michael D. Watkins, The First 90 Days

While Watkins' book is often a go-to suggestion for my leaving well clients, there are some important missing gaps in Watkins' framework. First of all, leaving - as a word or phrase - is not mentioned in the book's index. Additionally, one is then led to believe that the transition timeline for new hires is a mere few months after onboarding. Even with the most productive and effective onboarding in place, it can take up to one year before someone is fully settled into their new role, and efficiency is realized for their work. For executive level or cross-function / cross-department roles, that onboarding time can be upwards of two years.

Turnover costs can be incredibly disruptive. The Society for Human Resource Management (SHRM) reports that in hard costs, a company may spend 6 to 9 months of an employee's salary to replace them. In soft costs, the impact of an employee's departure is often felt across the organization, and not just in the HR offices.

As important as the transition plan is for those leaving, it is just as critical to replicate and prioritize the same steps in reverse for those joining the organization.

Organizational objectives and metrics inside social impact organizations are always some combination of social, environmental, and financial. Leaving Well as an organizational framework serves both the social (people) component and the financial aspects and prosperity index of your organization most directly. But, Leaving Well also serves the environmental component.

When transitions are managed well, the organization is more prepared and more likely to have a positive or symbiotic relationship with the mission, those being served, and the larger ecosystem or environment the organization is operating within.

What if leaving well was practiced as a leadership model?

"Great is the art of the beginning,
but greater is the art of ending"

HENRY WADSWORTH LONGFELLOW

The Problem in Organizations

The complexity of organizational leadership generates messy politics, the likelihood of missed metrics, misaligned outcomes, and abandoned impact.

Adding transition to the mix - whether or not you know it's happening or upcoming - brings a new intersection of challenges and struggle. It's a reality we will all encounter, many times in our professional lives, yet we aren't equipped to navigate it with intention.

Do these descriptions of the status quo resonate?

- There is a lack of intentional and thoughtful support during or after new hires.
- Finding reputable support specifically built for leaders entering or leaving transition spaces is hard.
- "Right Fit" is only based on current culture when new leaders are brought in. During times of transition, the organization often misses the opportunity to take into consideration the broad expertise and chemistry that a new leader possesses that they could bring into the team environment.

- Organizational expectations are not true to team needs, and are out of touch with on-the-ground realities for the work and impact needing to be accomplished.
- Leaders are not set up for success, and much precious time and energy is spent attempting to onboard.
- There is no organizational practice to internally practice leaving well.
- Leaders are left to navigate from one complex situation to the next without any time to process, heal, or seek support.

When companies and leaders fail to cultivate environments where leaving well is prioritized, employees will vote with their feet, leaving to seek better options where they will be embraced. The way in which an employee leaves (well or otherwise), can also impact the future reputation of your organization. When organizations prioritize leaving well, former employees will likely speak about their time and work in much more positive terms and in much more glowing ways. It's in everyone's best interest to practice leaving well.

When organizations equate their mis-hires to being wrong fit, a small pool of candidates, assumptions of being unqualified, it perpetuates a harmful and toxic untruth. To accomplish more right fit hires, seamless onboarding, achieved metrics, goals realized, & retention, then we MUST start with the process of leaving. How we bid the last person goodbye impacts the way we welcome the next. Many aspects of transitions are not in our control. What is within your control as an organizational leader is the choice to implement intentional and meaningful processes, and a culture that supports leaving well.

Leaving well, when practiced consistently, yields the following:

Continuity and Stability:

A successful organization is built on continuity and stability. When anyone departs, the sudden void can disrupt operations, team morale, and even donor and stakeholder confidence. Leaving well ensures a smooth transition, allowing the organization to continue its mission without major disruptions.

Preserving Trust and Reputation:

Nonprofit organizations rely heavily on the trust and goodwill of their stakeholders. By handling departures with integrity, transparency, and open communication, organizations can demonstrate their commitment to the organization and its stakeholders, enhancing its credibility and reputation.

Smooth Succession Planning:

Thoughtful leaders understand the importance of succession planning. By actively engaging your entire organization in the concept of leaving well, including the selection, hiring, and onboarding process, you will be given valuable insights and guidance that facilitate a seamless transition for the incoming leaders long into the future.

Nurturing Future Leaders:

One mark of an exceptional executive leader is their ability to develop and empower future leaders within the organization. By leaving well, current leaders create opportunities for emerging talent to step up and assume greater responsibilities. This not only strengthens the organization's leadership pipeline but also leaves a lasting legacy of growth and development.

Emotional and Psychological Impact:

The departure of an executive leader can trigger various emotions among those in the organization. A poorly managed departure can lead to big feelings and emotions (uncertainty, insecurity, and even resentment). By contrast, leaving well helps alleviate anxiety, maintain morale, and fosters a positive organizational culture during the transition period.

Knowledge Transfer and Documentation:

Executive leaders possess a wealth of knowledge, insights, and connections that are crucial for the organization's success. Leaving well involves sharing this institutional knowledge and ensuring that it is effectively transferred to the incoming leadership. By documenting processes, relationships, and strategies, departing leaders enable their successors to hit the ground running and build upon the organization's previous achievements.

The Ripple Effect:

Leadership sets the tone for the entire organization. When executive leaders leave well, they inspire a culture of professionalism, respect, and collaboration that permeates throughout the organization. This positive ripple effect cultivates an environment where future transitions are met with confidence and stability, attracting and retaining top talent and stakeholders.

Leaving well is an art executive leaders must not only master when transitioning from their organizations, but to also embed as a component of continuity, trust, and succession planning. A graceful departure not only reflects positively on their legacy but also ensures a seamless transition, nurtures future leaders, and preserves the organization's reputation and stability. Ultimately, leaving well is a testament to an executive leader's commitment to the greater good and their lasting impact on the organization's journey.

Leaving well is not just a nice idea, or a concept that sounds great in theory. It's a framework - a system - that you can implement within your organization today, whether you are just starting out, or you have years of legacy behind you.

Exploration of Scenarios and Leadership Transition Types

Picture your most dedicated nonprofit employee, walking into the office one morning to find out that their colleague is leaving. Panic ensues as their departure stirs up a whirlwind of uncertainty and stress. Any number of the following scenarios can begin to play out, immediately, when news of transitions gets out:

Scenario #1: *The Domino Effect*
The cascade of chaos and confusion begins, tasks are dropped, important information is lost, and everyone is left scrambling to pick up the pieces. A poorly managed transition can have a negative impact on team morale, productivity, and stakeholder relations.

Scenario #2: *The Great Knowledge Black Hole*
Transitions can feel like a black hole, sucking up all the knowledge and expertise accumulated by an employee over the years. Without a proper transition, that's exactly what happens when a valuable team

member departs. Enter frantic Googling, endless searches of your content management system, and much scratching of heads.

Scenario #3: *Ghost Town Syndrome*

This is the last thing you want your organization to resemble when employees leave. When transitions are handled poorly, employees may start feeling like they're stuck in a ghost town, where there's no sense of direction or support.

Scenario #4: *Positive Culture Cultivation*

A healthy transition is not just about logistics; it's about nurturing a positive organizational culture. When employees see that their colleagues are treated with respect and care during their transitions, it fosters a sense of trust and loyalty. On the other hand, if transitions are mishandled, it can create an atmosphere of fear and uncertainty.

~

We can categorize general types of transitions and leaving as: hot mess, murky middle, blank slate, impossible situations, and successful successions.

Hot Mess

In the first type of transition we find situations where someone in leadership has a sudden departure, whether from a resignation or termination, or from some type of massive failure where the leader is exited from the company. a serious illness or death of an executive/ leader will also generally result in a hot mess.

Murky Middle

This transition type occurs within organization structures that utilize co-director models, and other situations where there may be an overlap in leadership roles and duties. This type of transition also comes into play during the relocation of leadership, or when interim leadership is introduced.

Blank Slate

The blank slate situation often is felt at the beginning start up phase of a new organization, during a pivot of mission or programming, as well as when a new funding source is introduced to the organization.

Impossible Situation

While many of the situations named above feel challenging, the following moments are the pinnacle of impossible, including the sunset of an organization, when a scandal of personal or organizational nature happens, and when an icon in the community or beloved leader departs a well-known organization.

Successful Succession

The final type of transition includes planned departures and intentional transitions.

"When done well, openings and closings often mirror one another. Just as before your opening there should be a period of ushering, so with closings there is a need to prepare people for the end."

PRIYA PARKER

Buoys and Beacons

So how do we implement actions to move into a culture and practice of leaving well? Eight different navigation opportunities are offered to you here in a digestible way. You can skim over all eight, or read in detail based on your current needs. As you read, you'll notice a Buoy section and a Beacon section.

In the maritime world, buoys and beacons stand as resilient sentinels, providing invaluable assistance to seafarers, whether they are embarking on daring adventures or navigating well-trodden routes.

Buoys serve as indispensable markers in an otherwise featureless expanse of water. These resilient and carefully designed structures are strategically placed to alert watercraft to potential hazards, acting as steadfast guardians of safety. Beyond their role in alerting seafarers to danger, buoys also serve as mobile navigational aids, helping sailors chart their course amidst the vastness of the open waters. These floating beacons come in a variety of shapes and sizes, each bearing a specific meaning and purpose.

Beacons assume a more stationary role in the maritime landscape, and serve as unwavering navigational references, offering sailors a reliable point of reference amid the ebb and flow of tides. These beacons, often towering above the surrounding water, shine their guiding light across vast distances, beckoning ships towards safe harbors and guiding them along well-established routes.

The following eight sections will identify next steps of establishing leaving well as an organizational culture. Each section is referred to as a "navigation" and has both a beacon and a buoy.

The symbol of buoys refer to floating markers which alert watercraft to danger, or to mark a location and will offer you short, simple, and actionable suggestions. The symbol of beacons refer to markers that are set and fixed in the water, offering navigational support, and will provide deeper, culture-embedding suggestions.

Serve as a merchant of hope.
Serve as a beacon of possibility.

NAVIGATION SUMMARY
Translation, Norms, and Messaging

The concept of "river banks" is used as a metaphor for organizational integrity and boundaries. Just as river banks hold the water in place, organizational river banks define the values, norms, and communication standards that guide an organization. These river banks should be established and upheld during transitions to maintain stability and focus on the mission.

Leadership norms and modeling play a crucial role in shaping organizational culture and shared responsibility. Different leadership types offer different perspectives and strengths that can contribute to leaving well. Building messaging templates and assessing team dynamics are important steps in effectively communicating and implementing leaving well practices during transitions.

NAVIGATION SUMMARY
Relationship Management and Trust Bridges

The focus of this section is on relationship management and building trust bridges within an organization. It emphasizes the importance of sustained trust and relationships with all stakeholders, including volunteers and the community, during times of disruption and stress. The concept of leaving well is introduced as a strategic planning tool that brings mindfulness and intention to long-term organizational needs. Keeping resumes updated is encouraged as a way to stay connected to personal impact and identify growth opportunities.

The practice of stay interviews or engagement check-ins is suggested to foster a high-trust environment and increase employee retention. Managing relationships with external partners is also highlighted as a crucial aspect of transition planning. Overall, the section emphasizes the importance of trust, communication, and intentional relationship-building in creating a culture of leaving well.

NAVIGATION SUMMARY
Transition Planning

The section on transition planning focuses on the importance of having intentional plans in place for managing departures and onboarding new team members. It highlights the benefits of organization-wide transition planning, such as reducing stress and ensuring continuity. Socializing the concept of leaving well and embedding it into the organizational culture is encouraged. The paper chain analogy is used to illustrate how a positive or negative leaving experience can impact the organization.

Practical steps for creating a connection to a well-designed leaving well experience are suggested, along with the idea of going "above and beyond" during transitions. The importance of documentation, succession planning, and knowledge transfer is emphasized. The section concludes with suggestions for activities and duties to include in a transition plan, such as sticky note celebrations, gathering opportunities, and establishing a transition team or employee resource group.

NAVIGATION SUMMARY
Knowledge Transfer

The section on knowledge transfer emphasizes the importance of structured and comprehensive systems to ensure the transfer of institutional and cultural knowledge when employees leave an organization. It addresses the feelings of abandonment and upheaval during transitions and suggests involving the entire team in knowledge transfer exercises to create a culture of accountability and retention. Practical steps for effective knowledge transfer are provided, including creating an access document with passwords and work details, conducting quarterly check-ins, and prioritizing and documenting processes. The section encourages fostering discussions within departments to support documentation and completion of tasks.

NAVIGATION SUMMARY
Journey Maps

The section on journey maps highlights the importance of creating opportunities for teams to come together and gain a better understanding of the organization's purpose and customer journey, especially during periods of transition. It suggests utilizing mind maps, such as customer journey maps or user experience maps, to visualize the impact on clients or customers. The benefits of prioritizing this effort include increased connection to the work, insights into pain points and improvement opportunities, clarity about customer needs, and cross-departmental collaboration. The differences between customer journey maps and user experience maps are explained, and practical steps for implementing journey maps, from small group exercises to organization-wide projects, are provided.

NAVIGATION SUMMARY
Blueprint Redesign

The current leadership models often suffer from a scarcity mindset, where leaders feel a lack of time and resources, resulting in a limited number of leaders taking on too many roles. This scarcity mindset leads to imposter syndrome and weaponized incompetence among leaders. To address these issues, a rework of the leadership blueprint is suggested. This involves gaining clarity on the mission, reviewing and analyzing current systems, maximizing capacity and strategic connections, and assessing resource allocation.

Additionally, shifting the mindset of sustainability to view it as the responsible utilization of resources can create a healthier organizational environment. Cultural competence and intentional examination of the organizational blueprint are also important for improvement. Instead of complex restructuring, temporary work groups or committees can be implemented to address specific gaps. Lastly, embedding leaving well into cultural competence requires defining and communicating the culture, providing clear correlations, recognizing complexity, facilitating learning opportunities, involving staff, collaborating with others, normalizing training, and institutionalizing the language of learning well.

NAVIGATION SUMMARY
Legacy

The section on legacy emphasizes the importance of planning for our legacy in both personal and professional contexts. It discusses how neglecting to plan for our legacy can burden others and highlights the benefits of prioritizing our individual legacies while also caring for others. Practical examples, such as estate planning and leaving a workplace, illustrate the significance of leaving a positive legacy. The section encourages forward-thinking, intentional decision-making, and aligning actions with values to shape one's legacy and make a lasting impact. It emphasizes the importance of leaving well and creating a positive ripple effect for future individuals and organizations.

NAVIGATION SUMMARY
Care and Candor

The section on "Care and Candor" emphasizes the importance of cultivating a culture of radical candor in organizations, particularly in the nonprofit and service-based sectors. It suggests that all members of an organization share equal responsibility for the environment and culture, and shifting culture requires a collective effort. The concept of radical candor is defined as caring personally and challenging directly, fostering genuine connections and building trusting relationships. The section also references the book "Your Caring Heart" by Dr. Jaiya John, which explores the importance of mutual care and wellness among helping professionals and its positive impact on staff, teams, and overall organizational outcomes. It encourages individuals to plan and engage in conversations with specific goals in mind and to celebrate accomplishments while bidding farewell to past experiences.

NOTE TO THE READER:

Keep in mind your teams, and their capacity. As you identify with scenarios and examples that match your organizational needs, challenge yourself to choose a few buoys or beacons to implement within your teams.

Reminder

Buoys offer you short, simple, and actionable suggestions.
Beacons offer you deeper, culture-embedding suggestions.

Translation, Norms, and Messaging

What are your riverbanks?

In shaping your communication standards, voice and the power you wield with transition messaging, it's worth reflecting on what you'd like your organizational river banks to be. What pillars will be on your left and on your right? When processing and messaging upcoming transitions, what river banks will you choose to strongly hold?

Worth noting, your organizational river banks aren't obtrusive, or obnoxious. They fit in with the environment and no one really notices them, but they hold the river inside. Organizational river banks help your teams hold steady to the course, and maintain your mission, values, and your culture.

River banks allow you to "focus on the mission, not the details", and also support the absorption of disappointment and missed expectations easier during the upheaval of necessary endings and transitions.

It is crucial that we allow ourselves the grace and the space to change our minds or to let someone else's story change the way that we see something. Thinking of water, it is fluid and it has the ability to be ever changing. Your river banks don't change however. The water becomes the work, the day-to-day. It might be still one day or rushing the next. There might be rocks or debris ... or flood waters which spill over the banks. This is similar to a metaphor of doing upstream work of changing systems (especially in nonprofit / social work / advocacy work) at the source of the problem, instead of downstream work (rescuing the people harmed by systems and inequities out of the water over and over)

To find your own organizational river banks around transitions and leaving well, consider the following questions:

- What top four values does your organization operate by?
- Are boundaries easy for your organization to uphold?
- What guidelines does your organization have in place so you can do your best work?

In your organization, what are the norms about how work gets done? What are the norms about how joy and play enter work spaces? How does accountability and reconciliation happen? How does communication currently happen in your organization?

Leadership Norms, and Modeling
Everyone has the capacity to contribute and to choose responsibility. Everyone has the capacity to lead. Leadership is a choice, and it begins with one's willingness to be responsible for what is happening in one's world. What if the choice of responsibility generated a context of ownership and

self-authorship beyond the immediate task at hand? What if the responsibility of culture and norms at your organization was not solely on your shoulders?

Leaders-by-title and those with decision making power must have the awareness to notice what is needed in the moment when it comes to organizational health, as well as the agility to respond from a wide palette of creative choices rather than from an entrenched system of patterned and predictable reactions. In the grand scheme of responsibility and organizational culture, there can be a "co" inside of this responsibility.

Leadership development inside of the leaving well framework is about growing the size of the world for which one is able to be responsible. While all team members will not hold the same levels of accountability, it is still important to expand the capacity of all team members to embed an attitude of co-responsibility. The act of building trust bridges as often and in as many places as possible, across departments and projects allows for capacity expansion. Holding accountability to internal processes creates normalized muscle memory for repeated success.

Karen and Henry Kimsey-House offer the following examination of leadership components in their book Co-Active Leadership:

Leader **Behind** references those in serving and coaching roles, primarily committed to elevating and calling forth the brilliance of other people by believing in them and supporting them through deep listening, powerful questions and acknowledgement. These individuals are often more naturally focused on the protocols and future needs for the organization. As such, they can be effectively brought into the leaving well container to seek out improvement opportunities and other organizational needs as the process unfolds.

Leader **Beside** prioritizes collaboration and synergy, and these individuals consciously design their partnerships around a shared vision and intention, leveraging each other's strengths so that the whole being is greater than the sum of its parts. Leaders acting in this realm also balance openness and curiosity about the other person with a commitment to stand fully in their own authority.

Leader **in the Field** is a mindset of intuition and innovation, where leaders take responsibility for their world by slowing down and observing the deeper implications of what is happening, trusting their instinct and intuition beyond what is known and can be proved. These leaders often have their fingers on the pulse of the clients or customers served by your organization, and also have ties to the community.

Leader **Within** is less about actions that take place in the workplace in a visible way, and is more about the internal work of self-acceptance and self-authority, where individuals live with integrity in accordance with their personal values.

The work of modeling and normalizing a new culture around co-responsibility and this version of shared leadership for the purpose of leaving well will take time, and will also require an intentional effort to both acknowledge and champion the work and progress each and every time someone leaves, and each and every time someone joins the team. Celebrating achievements will become necessary, as will the willingness to consistently practice leaving well.

As the Leader **in Front** is referred to in the Kimsey-House book, it refers to the typical hierarchy of one decision maker, who steers the direction of the organization. This leader is wholly responsible for fostering connection with the people who are following them, and is primarily responsible to guide the clear purpose and mission of the work. This leader will be required to both step forward and sit down, often at the same time, in a classic situation of both/and. The idea of leaving well as a concept in your organization will rely on everyone to embed and prioritize it as culture. As the culture of leaving well is normalized in your organization, Leaders in Front will need to familiarize themselves with allowing for failure and a nuanced adoption of leaving well. Additionally, these leaders should prepare to support their team members in navigating the ebbs and flows as implementation practices are identified.

Buoy:
If you are actively in transition, consider taking some time to intentionally build out messaging templates to communicate to staff, the community you serve, media, donors, board of directors, and other stakeholders. Your messaging should consider the opportunity to uphold your brand reputation, as well as manage community expectations by directing the narrative about your organization's transitions

Beacon:
Looking back through the various leadership types referenced in this section, begin the process of examining your current team.

Which individuals naturally gravitate to each type of leadership? Where are your team's gaps when it comes to what will be necessary to implement leaving well? Where is your team leaning heavily to one side? Where can you develop and elevate innate qualities in individuals, to encourage them to step into these roles?

Relationship Management and Trust Bridges

A common refrain frequently heard from clients is one of wanting to prioritize the current disruption and stress." As clients begin to explore the full ecosystem of the organization, the leader realizes how important the sustained trust and relationships with all impacted persons (including volunteers and the community served by the organization) is to the process. Another ah-ha comes when we discuss leaving well as a strategic planning tool, not just to overcome immediate challenges, but also to bring mindfulness and intention around the long term needs for the organization

Each and every time I have managed a team, whether I'm the official manager, or I'm overseeing and managing a project, I level-set right at the beginning that ends are inevitable. We talk early on about the realities of leaving, acknowledging that we will all leave at some point in the project - whether that's because the work is completed, or because another organization called to us, or for other reasons. We can say, "Endings are inevitable, how can we plan now?"

After normalizing the concept and topic of leaving well, I offer time with folks to review resumes. I ask: "Have you updated it? Is your current work that you're doing on your resume?" Most times, the response I hear is a question wondering why on earth they would update their resume when they have no plans of leaving.

A few of the reasons I encourage everyone keep their resumes updated:

- Anything could happen - layoffs, reductions in force, a change in leadership, a decision you decide to make
- Reminding yourself of your current work helps you get crystal clear on your recent impact
- Offers a look into work that - as you realize it's missing from your resume - you may have set aside for other priorities
- Elevates moments for growth opportunities

Having an entire organization full of staff members with updated resumes is likely to do the opposite of what you might assume. Don't fall for the assumption that folks with up-to-date resumes will all start applying for roles at other organizations, or preparing to leave yours. Instead, this emboldens the value and culture of leaving well inside your organization, and helps everyone stay connected to their personal impact. Additionally, this exercise can be used to spot gaps or missed opportunities for growth and development within your organization.

Another component of this practice is building and securing trust bridges. One way to embed leaving well as a part of your culture is to integrate some of the common activities associated with an individual leaving into your day-to-day operations. Consider the concept of a stay interview. Also called "engagement check-ins", stay interviews serve as an opportunity to intentionally discuss real-time engagement, challenges, motivations, and desires for new work or development. Amy Mosher, chief people officer at isolved in Charlotte, N.C., *has seen a 10 percent increase* in annual employee retention over a period of two years, that she credits to engagement check-ins. Mosher says, "We feel the name conveys a high-trust environment versus a transactional one."

An organization's job isn't to empower and engage people, it is to remind people that they walk in the door with power, and then to create the conditions for them to exercise that power - as often as possible, and in a direction towards impact.

Exit interviews are for the benefit and purpose of the organization, specifically to ensure there are no unaired grievances or frustrations that might cause the exiting individual to become a bad apple. The contrary experience of regular and consistent stay interviews does wonders to creating a trust bridge.

"While the motivation is similar, our approach is to ensure that employees know that they are trusted and that they are empowered to share information about what is happening today and where they see themselves tomorrow," Mosher said. "Our managers tell us they feel more prepared for performance reviews as a result. By regularly checking in with employees specifically about engagement, they have a better idea of where their team can upskill next, where there might be a risk of churn and how to better serve their team. The completion of pulse surveys ... have increased. Our overall employee engagement scores [have increased] by 8 percent."

Consistency is key for this concept, as is the importance of instituting this concept across your entire organization. "We're now seeing happier employees who are eager to come or log in to work and contribute," said Kate Grimaldi, senior director of enterprise talent strategy for Paylocity in Chicago. "Managers have become more effective because they know what employees care about personally and professionally, and what really motivates someone to remain with us. These discussions have led to exciting new assignments, new learning paths, or just improved relationships with employees and their direct managers, which has a real impact on retention."

While leaving well is not solely or primarily about employee retention, retention ends up being an incredible by-product. Your organization's focus on improving the employees' work experience can shift a workplace culture from feeling disconnected, detached, and void of felt impact. When a trust bridge is clearly established between all layers of an organization, feelings of being valued and engagement increase exponentially.

The word conversation derives from the Latin *conversare,* "to turn about with". What if every conversation were an opportunity to turn with someone, toward something?

Keep in mind that during stay interviews or engagement check-ins, you will need to foster a culture of giving radically honest feedback, and grow your own capacity (and that of your managers) to receive feedback in return. Pause, repeat the feedback and then thank them for being honest. Then internally work on how you can implement and act on the feedback.

In addition to managing and building relationships that are strongly connected to a leaving well culture, it is also important to manage the relationship and trust bridge with your external partners, which includes clients, the community, funders, investors, board of directors, and other stakeholders. Communication and messaging during transitions is a necessary relationship management, which will be covered in the section on Transition Planning.

Buoy:
Creating a regular occurrence where staff updates their resumes to help your organization stay relevant and connected to your impact. Another buoy is creating an environment to note and celebrate your employees' Worthy Work. Worthy Work is an exercise and practice of noticing the sometimes small acts that add up to impactful work. Worthy Work may include offering support to another team member, finding a finance loophole, or finalizing an important presentation for the organization.

Beacon:
Inject and embed the concept of stay interviews into your organization. Offer these questions to managers, allowing customization based on their departments and specific team members. Suggested questions may include:

- How do you feel your work currently connects to your own personal values?
- What is the most satisfying component of your current work?
- What is the recent project or body of work you're most proud of?
- What keeps you working here?

- What do you look forward to when you come to work each day?
- What do you like most or least about working here?
- If you could change something about your job, what would that be?
- What would make your job more satisfying?
- How do you like to be recognized?
- What talents are not being used in your current role?

Transition Planning

Succession planning and standard operating procedures (SOPs) are on everyone's to-do list, but they never actually get done. Part of this is because the work of our organizations takes priority, as well as the reality that the systematic approach to documenting processes is not something that comes naturally to most staff, let alone knowing how to spot gaps in service delivery and process.

An organization contacted me while in the midst of the departure of their executive director. Their primary goal was to manage expectations during the departure. During their intake session, we identified their underlying motivation for doing this work was also to reduce stress for their team members and protect organizational continuity. Both of those reasons closely align with the benefits of organization-wide transition planning.

One of the biggest sources of frustration, lost time, squandered efficiency, and energy comes from a lack of an intentional transition plan. There are a myriad of formats for transition plans, but at the bare minimum should include a loose framework for offboarding and onboarding (this includes staff, volunteers, and board members!), as well as information about your business cycles (whether projects, grants, funding, events, or campaigns).

In my childhood, we made paper chains in order to count down the days to important celebrations or happenings. Small strips of paper with the ends attached to each other, forming circles, with each subsequent circle looping into the last, forming a chain. As employees leave organizations, they will form a proverbial paper chain, and it can either be a positive experience or a negative one. It will either be "One more day done, thank goodness." or on each paper chain link, there could be an intentional component of a leaving well transition plan.

First ask these two questions:

- How do you want your exiting employees to feel as they leave?
- How do you want the stayers to feel as the transition occurs?

Then work in reverse over the course of time that you have remaining, identifying practical and manageable daily items and tasks to create a connection to a well designed leaving well experience.

In addition to the recaptured energy, transparency and clarity that comes with a transition plan, you will simultaneously be building a culture where people go "above and beyond" when leaving. Inside organizations that prioritize leaving well, more employees will opt to expand their transition beyond the traditional two weeks notice.

Embedding leaving well into your organization during a transition, or in the time following a recent one, offers a memory recall, and multiple points of view to seek a new way of operating for the future.

Buoy:
Intentionally plan some activities to correlate with the few days after an employee gives notice. You can decide to implement one or all, but the simple act of acknowledging this person and their contribution to the organization goes a long way.

— Sticky Note Celebrations:
Ask your team to leave a sticky note at the workspace of the departing team member. Encourage them to leave a quote, or a song they are reminded of. They could also leave a sticky note sharing what they've brought to the team, or an important memory.

— Gathering:
If your team regularly gathers around food, or at a certain location, consider making space in your work week for an opportunity for the team to commune over food or another enjoyable activity.

— Communication:
Examine your communication standards around notifying the organization about a departing team member. Is it better for that notice to come from HR, or from the person's manager? What could it look like if the person departing was able to write their own 2-3 sentence notification to the team? Be sure to include their final date of employment, and consider injecting an acknowledgement of the departing employee's contribution to the team.

Beacon:

Consider identifying one individual or a small team to manage transitions.This should involve both providing structure and support before, during, and after transition takes place. For larger organizations, consider establishing a more formalized transition team or create an employee resource group (ERG). Duties to consider including for this purpose include a team lead, a particular focus on database / documentation:

Transition Team Lead (responsible for overall project management)

Project Lead / Transition Specialist (responsible to identify project activities needed before, during, following transition)

Database Administrator

Ops and Systems

Project Support / Help Desk

Consider the following as minimum actions for your transition plan:

- Discussion between successor and new manager of new position, accountabilities, and expectations
- Training requirements for new position discussed and executed or in progress
- Effective date and probation period established and agreed upon by successor for new position
- Finalized support role of incumbent over course of transition period - if applicable

- Provided relevant business issues information, including projects, initiatives, and tasks

- Provided direct report information and project details

- Provided location of pertinent documents and records, as well as lists of pertinent contacts

- Communication and notification to external contacts, suppliers, clients, etc

- Communication and notification to internal contacts, direct reports, and committee members

Knowledge Transfer

A common obligation or burden held by those departing an organization is the feeling that they need to "get everything out and on paper" about their role, duties, projects, and work they've been tasked with during their time at the organization. They have a desire to intentionally provide knowledge transfer, but without structure and a comprehensive system in place, the natural reality is that the transfer of institutional and cultural knowledge falls by the wayside.

During any period of transition, it is common for there to be a feeling of abandonment and upheaval. It's also very easy for those who remain, to feel that the transition is somehow personal. During these moments of the environment shifting, there are powerful ways to acknowledge these feelings and use the time to involve the full team of employees to facilitate knowledge transfer.

Examine the structure of your organization, first looking at the role, duties, and responsibilities of those in transition. What are the systems required to be retained and maintained through the leaving? What processes and procedures need to be shored up and built into a documented resource? How can this all be adequately and efficiently documented?

Practicing the act of accountability to each other and to the organization can help team members remember that the actual work must also have a stickiness and retention component. Involving the entire team in a knowledge transfer exercise can transform the effort from stagnant or a struggle, to something that embodies muscle memory and a habit or practice.

Some of the key components of a solid knowledge transfer include:

- the title or name of all projects or programs
- client contacts and details
- details for all individuals with project knowledge
- project status
- delivery timeline
- location of working notes and files
- any concerns or delays
- funding or investment details
- additional information and notes

Buoy:

Create a simple access document, which includes noted passwords, login credentials, and a list of details for the work that each employee currently utilizes in their day-to-day. Ask each employee to utilize a template for consistency, and add a calendar item across your organization for a quarterly check-in and update of the access document.

Beacon:

As you begin to embed the culture of leaving well into your organization, begin operating your team meetings towards regular knowledge transfer. Begin the work of identifying prioritized processes that need to be documented. A bonus opportunity is to foster discussions in each department that allow for team members to have the space to raise projects and to do items that have been stuck or stagnant. This provides an opportunity to shore up that work and support the embedded work of documentation and completion of processes.

Journey Maps

At the beginning of one notable project, a common theme throughout the organization was that very few people understood or had a solid knowledge of what other team members were responsible for. Additionally, they lacked a baseline understanding of the overall organization's purpose, beyond their specific department.

This phenomenon is more common than you might imagine. Add in the inevitable reality of transition, and any team unity and togetherness in existence is often the first thing to fall by the wayside.

Consider using the reality of transition to intentionally create opportunities for your team to come together.What better opportunity than to examine your customer or client journey. Organizations typically think about their customer or client too infrequently, yet the outcomes intended to serve them can be impacted during transitions in your organization.

1. Have your department leads and managers create the first draft, to be presented to the full organization for input and feedback

2. Create them together, via multiple workshops with various team members

There are many benefits to your organization prioritizing this effort, including:

- Increased connection to the work and greater understanding of the mission, vision, and purpose of the organization
- Elevated insights about pain points, gaps, improvement opportunities across the organization
- Clarity gained about the customer's needs and motivations
- Opportunities rising for efficiency, consistency, satisfaction, referrals, etc.
- Team cohesion around decision making, leadership
- Funding and investment needs clarity
- Evaluation and process improvement
- Cross-departmental collaboration and teamwork opportunities

There can be some confusion about the differences and similarities between a customer journey map and a user experience map. Many folks use these terms interchangeably, and while that's not a drastic problem, it is helpful to understand the main differences:

User Experience Map:

A broader representation of the general experience of your organization, not tied to a specific customer or product / service. UX maps often also detail the steps to complete a specific task or goal, typically contained inside one department or product function. UX maps are created from the perspective of what the organization has in place even prior to a person becoming a customer, and can include competition or larger market information.

Customer Journey Map:

A view of the customer experience across the entire organization, which includes departmental interactions and multiple touchpoints. This is often created by compiling a set of actions into a timeline, from "start to finish" as the customer interacts with your organization. This map is created from the perspective of the customer and will include various stages of interaction, as well as "persona based" thoughts and emotions that may overlay each action and stage.

Buoy:

Set aside a portion of an upcoming department meeting and ask members to use a piece of paper to draw their understanding of their customer or client's journey and experience. Encourage them to only add 5-6 key moments along their map.

Offer time for small group discussion, and ask the team members to share their maps with each other. Where are there similarities and differences across everyone's hand drawn examples? Use this exercise to identify gaps and opportunities in the delivery of product and work inside your individual departments.

Beacon:

Implementing an organization-wide journey map for your customer or client is a more intense project, but with a few key folks leading it, this can yield an amazing and incredible set of insights. I've had success helping organizations do this exercise digitally, using a tool like Lucid or Visio. Other groups prefer to utilize a large white board with a set location in someone's office or in a main area of the building. In one setting, we used labeled magnets (one label type per department), and as we mapped the customer's journey, each person in the organization came through to self-identify where they felt they (or their department) had responsibility and ownership over that section of the map.

Using the examples shared above, look intentionally for breaks and gaps. Use the final product as a way to explore areas for improvement, streamlining, effectiveness, and where it makes sense, efficiency measures. Do not be surprised if this exercise brings about questions such as, "Should we keep doing this specific thing?" or "Why do we do this certain thing in this specific way?". Be open to exploring alternatives!

"Current leadership models pair scarcity of time with a mindset of scarcity of resources, which result in a smaller-than-necessary number of leaders holding a ton of urgent and very necessary roles. Leaders often don't know what we're doing, how to contribute, or what our value is outside of constant production."

adrienne maree brown, Emergent Strategy

Blueprint Redesign

Many leaders-by-title have the same imposter complex as other members of the team, regardless of their role in the organization, and in some cases weaponized incompetence is displayed as a result of the scarcity mindset.

One solution to this challenge to consider is a rework of the leadership blueprint at your organization. Reviewing your capacity, the structural relationship with your network, and existing strategic connections will maximize opportunities to navigate transitions.

Regarding capital, where in your organization do you have all resources necessary to accomplish your mission? Where do you need additional capital? What resources feel lacking or misaligned? Stay interviews are a great opportunity to identify underutilized skill sets and talents. When the results are analyzed methodically and thoughtfully, these insights can lend themselves well to help fill any gaps in your organization's capacity and/or capital.

Sustainability is often harmfully operationalized solely as a metric and method to keep something going and moving forward. Consider a shift in mindset. View sustainability as the method of harvesting resources, or utilizing resources such that they are not depleted or permanently damaged. Consider the difference in the felt environment of your organization with this as a norm.

Instead of continuing in a business-as-usual mindset, choose a reset from the current transition. Invite new conversations about your current sustainability measures, leadership structure, and organizational capacity.

Another component of reworking your organizational blueprint involves taking an intentional look at your cultural competence. Cultural competence is a developmental process that evolves over an extended period, and will take some time and effort. Both individuals and organizations are at various levels of awareness, knowledge, and skills along the cultural competence continuum, and the analysis of your current spectrum allows you to find improvement opportunities.

Cultural competence also involves transforming one's knowledge levels about organizational frameworks. Competency in this area allows the integration of concepts like leaving well to become standards, policies, practices, and attitudes that embed into the foundation of your organization. Ultimately this expands the capacity of your organization, and the effectiveness of sustainability pillars.

Buoy:
If you identify important gaps in the realm of capacity and/or capital, you may feel tempted to start shuffling the roles of your people. However, instead of undergoing a complicated restructure in your organization, consider instead implementing the concept of temporary work groups or committees. Perhaps you have a training gap and the required elements of training have long been a need for

the organization. If, during the exploration of your current capital, you discover that some of your team has previously designed, programmed, and delivered training, consider a short-term project where they can contribute to the effort of solving that problem.

Beacon:

Embedding long-term leaving well cultural competence includes, but is not limited to, the following considerations:

1. Define and communicate the leaving well culture broadly and transparently.

2. Provide clear correlations between organizational values, underlying client needs, and the value-add of leaving well.

3. Recognize complexity in implementation and maintenance.

4. Facilitate learning opportunities during the initial implementation, and socialize to stakeholders and the community for maximum impact.

5. Involve the staff and team members in defining and addressing implementation needs.

6. Collaborate with other agencies and offer peer learning opportunities, especially inside of cross-sector opportunities.

7. Normalize train–the-trainer and internal staff training.

8. Institutionalize the language of learning well and socialize regularly and consistently.

Additionally, as you familiarize yourself with the leaving well concept and rework your own blueprint, you can begin socializing it, simply by naming it. Once you've named it, and you begin signaling its importance, culture embedding can begin. A simple way to implement this is to say the words: "As we navigate this employee's departure, I would like our organization to prioritize leaving well." Let your teams be curious and embrace it in their own way. You can continue by saying, "What this means for me, and what it might mean for you is ..." There will be interest, intrigue, and at the very minimum, staff members will go about their normal operations. In the best of scenarios, you will start to witness a narrative shift as the concept ripples into the environment of your organization.

Legacy

What are we asking others to do because we didn't plan for our legacy? The importance of planning for our legacy exists in both the workplace and our personal spaces. In a professional space, when there is no legacy preparation, it places the burden for a future absence on the shoulders of those who stay behind. Those who remain must maintain their own work as well as preparing for a new hire. It is possible however, to prioritize our own individual legacy, and protect the legacy of our organizations, while also caring for each other, and the community.

A practical example of this can be found in the routine space of end-of-line planning. I did not fully understand how important this was until I was asked to manage my uncle's estate. There were so many situations where I said, "If only he had done …" Part of his legacy could have been the act of organizing his life and assets so all that was left for his loved ones to do was celebrate and grieve, instead of scramble, stress, and navigate chaos.

So that all you have to do as part of one's legacy is celebrate, grieve, and remember.

Legacy in the workplace can be a path set forth in advance and with intention. We can flip the switch and toggle forward thinking, to allow us to lay out a runway: What do you want your legacy to be? How do you want it to align with your values? Once you've begun to ask those questions, you can start pulling in whatever you're working on. A project. A team you're working with.

When thinking about the legacy of our life while looking back, we can start to identify what stays true through the navigation of different situations, projects and experiences. It's very common to then realize what the common denominators are, the red thread that runs throughout. Normalizing the pivot of this line of thinking to the future enables us to map proactive decisions and choices as they relate to individual legacy.

Since we are all going to leave one day, what if we looked at our remaining time as intentional and purposeful? In this perspective, you can almost design what people will say about you and about your impact. We can influence things like this today. You can design what people will say in the future about your organization, your leadership, the impact of your work, in the present.

How do you want your organization and your leadership to be known? At our core, we all crave a place where we belong, and we all crave to be known for who we truly are.

As I've worked alongside various organizations over the last decade, I've had an outside perspective on the trauma that happens as people leave organizations and projects, or as people try so hard to valiantly show up every day for their work. There's often no overarching culture, no purpose, no river banks, guideposts. There's no legacy.

I realized quickly that often this happens when we forget our values, or forget why we say "yes" to the project or job in the first place. When we don't remember those things, when we are lacking river banks, buoys, or beacons to guide our work, our legacy falls apart.

Someone called me recently saying they were leaving their job in the next six to nine months. They were tired and felt they'd done all they could at their organization. My first recommendation was that they write out everything they initially wanted to accomplish when starting their job. The next recommended step was to look at what had already been completed compared to what remained on the list. One last step was to take note of the remaining projects and lingering tasks that most resonated with their desired legacy. With this simple method complete, those next six to nine months became so laser focused on those identified projects and tasks. It also served to answer the question of how they wanted to be known as they exit. The exercise allowed them to stay connected - energetically and emotionally - prioritizing both their own needs and the needs of the organization while navigating the upcoming departure and timeline.

In the physical example of leaving well when moving home, our family always makes sure we go back to our favorite places. We make sure that we go back to say goodbye to our favorite wait staff. We make sure that we take photographs of the things that really matter to us. These acts can also be applied to the leaving well concept in our careers, our professional lives.

When we liken this concept to the act of leaving a physical place, part of your legacy can also be built in the way that you bid adieu to the relationships and outcomes you were tasked with. if you don't intentionally say, "thank you", you risk leaving a place with unfinished business. Leaving well changes the quality of an employee's remaining time, and instead of being bogged down by operational demands, your engagement with the remaining work shifts.

Since we know that leaving is inevitable, what are the small things we can do to help protect imprint and legacy?

Buoy:
Swap "how many days left" for "You have this much time left. What can we do today?" This pivot shifts everything.not only that, but this becomes an opportunity for modeling behavior. The ripple effect of leaving well resonates with the folks that stay, whether they know it or not, and they'll pick up on that same energy. It also helps them welcome the next person in a much more positive way.

Another simple injection is to seize opportunities to talk candidly about the legacy of those who have left in the past. Examine their contributions and share them at an upcoming team meeting. Reflect on opportunities in your own work life to proactively design your own legacy, even as you process and grieve the exit of others.

Where are the opportunities to contribute to the future health of the organization?

Beacon:

If you have a bit more time to devote to this container, the most important way you can focus on your impact is to revisit your personal and organizational values.

From a comprehensive list of common values, choose the top three to four values that you identify with for yourself or your organization, and pull them into a living document. Start to identify how those overlap, and how you already see those in your day-to-day work space.

One of my values is kindness. If kindness is a value for me, am I bringing that to work every day? This sounds rudimentary, but a kindness value for me lives out when I schedule a meeting: I make sure that I have a pre-read. If a recipient doesn't already know about my organization, I include a link in the calendar invite, and add the agenda that we're going to talk about. I only schedule for 45 minutes so that colleagues have time for a bio break in the midst of packed days.

The feedback I receive from clients then flows forth from these deliberate actions, in a way that reflects positive intention. Find those values that you identify with for your life and then start to see how you can attach them to your work.

Think about the things that you were excited about when you first took the role or when you first were asked to apply for the job. What were the things that were so exciting? Oftentimes, we lose sight of those as the day-to-day operations take over.

Remembering those things: can you invite them back? Can you invite the excitement back? What are the things that felt too big, those that someone told you you couldn't accomplish, that you eventually set to the side? Revisit those, because those can also be legacy.

This is leadership by preparation.

This is legacy and imprint.

Care and Candor

Fingers are often pointed at executive directors, board of directors, and funders, when it comes to criticisms of the environment and culture in nonprofit and other service-based organizations. However, all members of an organization - whether staff, volunteer, or outside stakeholders - have an equal amount of responsibility for the environment and culture. How then can we inject that responsibility mindset into our organizations?

In Radical Candor by Kim Scott, she defines radical candor as caring personally, and challenging directly.

Caring personally is the antidote to robotic professionalism and managerial arrogance. Caring personally is not about memorizing birthdays and names of family members. It's about acknowledging we are all people with lives and aspirations that extend beyond those related to our shared work. It's about finding time for real conversations, learning what's important to people, about what makes us want to get out of bed in the morning and go to work - and what has the opposite effect. Challenge directly helps build trusting relationships, to enable a reciprocal dynamic.

I will state clearly here that I've yet to work in or with an organization that has had the safety, or organizational norm to hold space for radical candor. At the same time, I will offer that we - one at a time, in each of our organizations - must begin taking the posture of "we decide, we shift culture, we create transformation".

"Health and wellness must happen in the workforce, first. We are responsible for each other's wellness, regardless of position. Staff are not powerless, but powerful in their duty to support and care for themselves and their leadership. Whatever we are practicing and experiencing, we will administer. Service capacity is an outcome of investment in workforce wellness. We can keep looking for a magic potion to change our reality, or we can simply take better care."
- Dr. Jaiya John

Written by Dr. Jaiya John, the book Your Caring Heart: Renewal for Helping Professionals and Systems is on my highly recommended list for frontline staff, outreach providers, those in human services, or as Dr. Jaiya describes:

A helping professional is defined as someone who provides support, directly or indirectly, to others who are in significant need. If what you do affects vulnerable lives, this book is for you. And, if you are an administrator, an executive, then you, my friend, should care about agency, worker, and leader wellness because this absolutely determines the bottom line (fiscal), the top line (political), and the real line (social, generational outcomes).

In Dr. Jaiya's book, he addresses the benefits of mutual care which include:

- Staff feel safer and more relaxed

- Staff operate at a higher level

- Staff are freed to apply their gifts

- Less days lost to unwellness

- Greater efficiency and higher morale

- More trust, effective communication and understanding

- Less misunderstanding and conflict

- Staff and leadership feel more empowered, validated, and supported

- Stronger teams and teamwork

- Minimized impact of stress and trauma

- Less staff and leadership turnover

- Stronger culture and continuity of values

As you read that list, what else comes to mind for you? Which of those realities feel the most aligned to the vision you have for your organization?

Buoy:

Plan your specific goals for the conversation. Some examples that can start with "I want to leave the conversation having said ....."

- That I care about the person

- That I appreciate _____

- That the project is over, but I want the professional relationship to continue

- The explicit reasons that the project or relationship is over

Beacon:

Imagine a time capsule. What would you put in it, knowing that so much has been invested? Tell stories about those items, those memories, those accomplishments. Celebrate the past, say goodbye to them.

"I knew that they had had so much invested in it that if we did not allow them to have a proper good-bye, they would not be able to move on. People can't really disinvest themselves and move on unless they say goodbye to what has been."

MOE GIRKINS

Grief Mindset and Navigating Loss

Change is inevitable, and so are necessary endings. We naturally fear change because of the unknown. We also fear change because of the disruption that occurs. However, healthy and potent opportunities for growth and foundational structure exist inside of transitions.

- Why do we avoid endings?

- The current situation is what we know

- Fear of the unknown

- Desire to do no harm and not hurt anyone

- Conflict avoidance

- Floundering is uncomfortable

- Lack of understanding about how "do endings well"

As organizations begin collectively normalizing endings, instead of focusing on them as a negative, more and more will accept that while they may be painful, endings are a gift.

"I knew that they had had so much invested in it that if we did not allow them to have a proper good-bye, they would not be able to move on. People can't really disinvest themselves and move on unless they say goodbye to what has been."
-Moe Girkins

The only energy you can invest is available energy. To make it available, you have to withdraw it from something else. The technical psychological term for that is "to decathect". Cathexis is the investment of mental or emotional energy in a person, an object, or an idea. So decathexis is the process of taking it back. The only way to do that is to grieve for what has been invested in before, so you can move forward. *(Necessary Endings)*

Grief means looking the reality right in the face and dealing with it, the reality that [whatever this is] is over. Finished.

Grief also means to prepare for what is next, because I am finishing what is over.

The American Psychological Association says it is the anguish experienced after significant loss, usually the death of a beloved person. Grief often includes physiological distress, separation anxiety, confusion, yearning, obsessive dwelling on the past, and apprehension about the future.

Systems that don't hold space and permission for grieving become depressed places of chronic, unreleased grief. Working with others in your cause brings grief. People change their positions, are promoted, leave the job. Formal leaders transition away. Those left behind feel abandoned, even lost. We grieve these various relationships and their influence, which is a good thing. A reflection of the meaning the relationships have to us. A testimony to the bonds and journey. Healthy grieving celebrates the memories, even the challenging ones. It is a storytelling river that goes on for years. Our relationships become legend, and in becoming legend, serve as mortar for the foundation of a relational system. -Dr. Jaiya John

When thinking about the process of navigating through grief, the idea of metabolism comes to mind. Metabolic was borrowed from German metabolisch, first borrowed from Greek metabolikós "changeable, subject to change," and connects with transition, to pivot, to turn about. The act of metabolizing takes one kind of energy and turns it into something usable.

To metabolize endings, consider these questions:

- What was good about the experience?
- What can you use as you go forward?
- What new skills did your team collectively attain?
- What modeling or knowledge did you witness and absorb?
- What needs to be corrected or shifted?
- What was not good about the experience?

> "Change can be a tender, poignant thing if we nurture each other in grieving. Grieving is not a distraction from work. Grieving together makes life, and work, a warmer river."

DR. JAIYA JOHN

Take the lessons and learnings, and consciously make them a part of your organization. Cement and bake them into your culture. Focus on them regularly so that they are not lost. Allow a foundation and culture of leaving well to become your organization's ecosystem, its cells and bones. Let this culture become your character and what you are known for.

"Your next step always depends on two ingredients: how well you are maximizing where you are right now, and how ready you are to do what is necessary to get to the next place. And sometimes that depends on ending some of what is happening today. For the right tomorrow to come, some parts of today may have to come to a necessary ending."

DR. HENRY CLOUD

Final Thoughts

"Three points of vulnerability exist in your
work life: when you enter, while you exist,
and as you leave. As you enter, you bring
both beauty and baggage. Your greatest
duty at work is not to survive but to affect
the climate."

DR. JAIYA JOHN

So what can you do about all of this? In your position in the organization, whether as the executive director, a managing leader, or a director level, you care about the people you work with, that is a given. It's also a given that you are significantly assessed and benchmarked against the optimization of resources, both fiscal and human. The bottom line impact of leaving well is substantial and caring well for each other must be practiced and ritualized so that it becomes a habit.

Care Personally:

- Start a conversation with your direct report, or someone on your board of directors, or a peer / colleague, and ask them to share a bit about their life story.

- Share any points of their experience and history that connect to the mission of your work, or the values of your organization.

- Name the impact and contribution to the legacy and system change.

Mutual Care:

- If your organization has recently had a transition, or one is looming, offer to host a casual gathering of your peers for a send off, or a debrief if the person has already moved on. From Dr. John: "craft an agenda of laughter, cleansing tears, remembrance, broadening of perspective, and lightening of heart."

- Make a list of the amazing teachings, skills, value, and culture components that you feel that person could "take with them" as they leave.

- Where are there gaps, as that person transitions from the project or organization? Where are the opportunities for those who are staying to take up those identified items?

"Over 4000 people have worked on this mission. There's no one person who can really get their arms around the whole thing and say 'I understand everything about this vehicle.'" -Steve Squyres (who led the Mars Exploration Rover Mission)

Just as one person is not wholly responsible for the outcomes and success of projects and organizational impact, one person leaving is not the end of the world or a disaster for your projects or organization. However, ONE person can start the revolution and shift in our systems around caring for one another.

I challenge you to find the opportunities to care personally and care well for each other during transition, identify the areas where you need to decide, where you need to shift culture, and where you need to act in order to create transformation.

"It's time for each of us to look ourselves in the mirror and finally admit that we are playing a powerful role in the system. We can either exist outside of our power, or choose to decide, to shift culture, and to create transformation."

NAOMI HATTAWAY

Noticing our impact takes on a different reality when we realize that others are watching. Not only are your employees watching, but other organizations, possible candidates and future employees are too. Think of a pebble falling into a pond. There is an initial impact as the pebble hits the water, but what follows is a much larger impact as ripples issue out from the pebble, sometimes even lapping against the opposite shore. Expand your awareness to include the work beyond your own individual experience. When we practice leaving well, we are able to "rest in the joy of service and the inherent knowledge that we are creating our world together every day in a way that is important, connected, and real" even when the relationship may no longer be connected by the same payroll company.

If one advances confidently in the direction of his dreams, and endeavors to live the life which he has imagined, he will meet with a success unexpected in common hours. If you have built castles in the air, your work need not be lost; that is where they should be. Now put the foundations under them." -Thoreau

In putting the foundations under those "castles in the air", you inevitably and intentionally design your legacy, and that of your organization. You are putting the ripple out into the water, taking care of your imprint and affecting the climate.

"Growth itself demands that we move on. Without the ability to end things, people stay stuck, never becoming who they are meant to be, never accomplishing all that their talents and abilities should afford them." -Dr. Henry Cloud

---

Allow things to die. Allow them to end. Allow people to leave. Allow what doesn't belong to fade. Allowing and surrendering creates more space for what is meant to be here at this time.

SYLVESTER MCNUTT III

ACKNOWLEDGEMENTS

Much appreciation to these individuals for their time reading, editing, and incredibly useful feedback:
Aimee Latta
Althea Soover
Emma Davidson-Tribbs
Regina Anaejionu
Sarah Johnson
Stu Davidson-Tribbs
Ursula Rafer

ABOUT THE AUTHOR

Naomi Hattaway's deep understanding of nonprofit and organizational spaces spans affordable housing, homelessness prevention, marketing, strategy, and communications. She brings Leaving Well to organizations and individuals leaders, and consults on inclusive program design for nonprofits, affordable housing, and communications. She also owns 8th & Home, a network matching folks on the move with Realtors who chase communities not commissions.

After living across the US, her family moved to India where they lived for three years, and she learned to thrive in the midst of chaos. Following one year in Singapore, they moved back to the US and have traipsed their way through Florida, Virginia, Ohio, and Nebraska, and currently living back in Florida.

Naomi's practice of leadership and implementation of the Leaving Well concept combines strategic visioning, organizational development, and community care. She delivers a deep commitment to equitable practices, a willingness to have tough conversations, strong project management and facilitation skills, and compassion and generosity to every interaction and facet of her work.

As a speaker, she has delivered keynotes at Union Pacific's Law and Risk conference, and the Families in Global Transition conference in both Washington DC and The Hague, Netherlands. She has spoken at conferences and presented workshops, as well as speaking engagements with Creative Mornings Omaha and CreativeMornings Field Trips.

Her Leaving Well clients applaud her ability to navigate workplace transitions, offering clarity, practices that stick, and guidance that supports the entire organization.

For more information or to connect with Naomi, visit **NaomiHattaway.com/next**